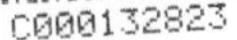

GOOD sex GUIDE

Thorsons
An imprint of HarperCollins*Publishers*
77-85 Fulham Palace Road,
Hammersmith, London W6 8JB

Published by Thorsons 1995
1 3 5 7 9 10 8 6 4 2

A catalogue record for this book is available from the British Library

ISBN 0 7225 3329 2

Executive Editor: *Lorraine Dickey*
Art Direction: *Zoë Maggs*
Project Editor: *Lol Henderson*
Photography: *Ken Niven*

Printed in Italy

THE POCKET

GOOD SEX GUIDE

YOUR SHORT CUT TO
SEXUAL ECSTASY

Thorsons

Dr David Delvin

CONTENTS

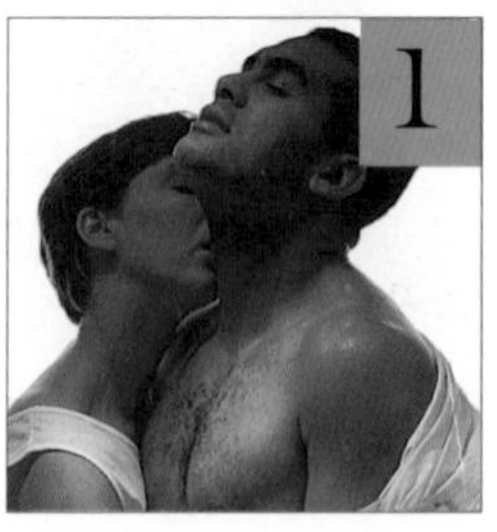

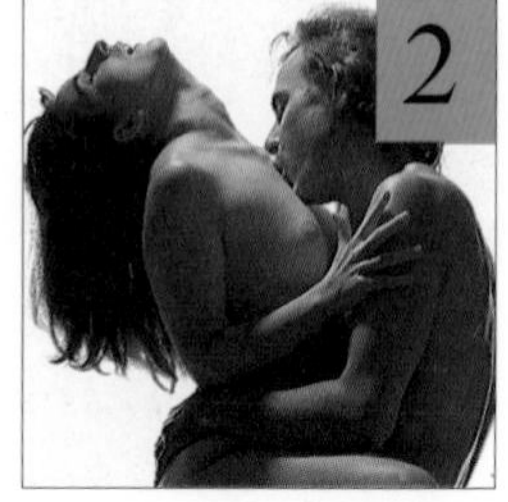

3

4

5

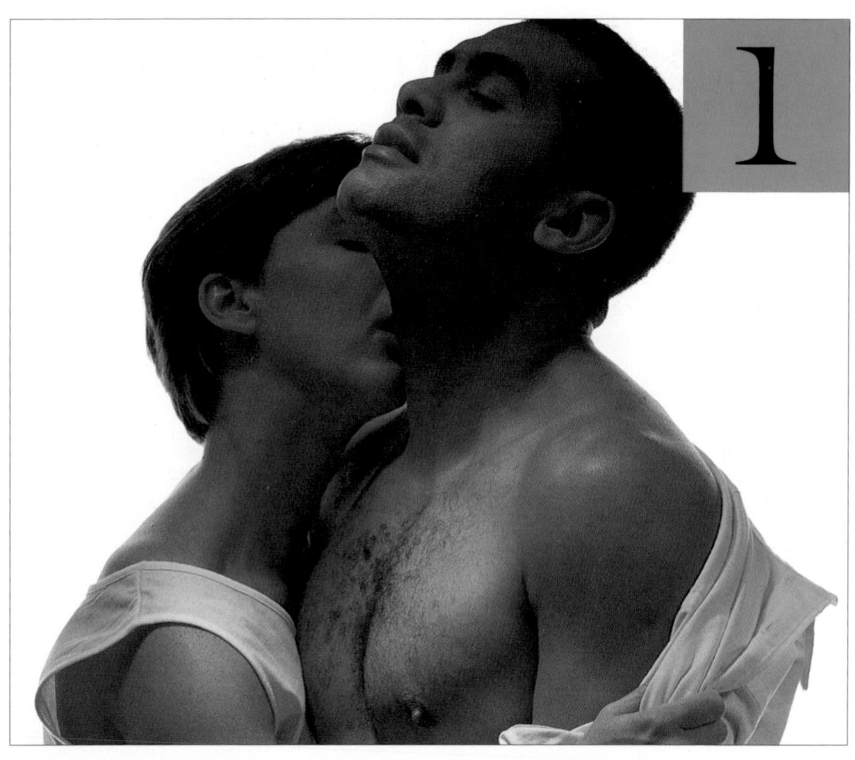

1

CHAPTER ONE

Sexual Performance

Today, society is preoccupied with the sexual performances of both men and women alike. Although this performance-oriented nonsense, in which people are judged by how well they score in bed, has no relevance to real life or having a good relationship, sexual performance is still sometimes rated according to a list of misconceived prerequisites.

for men:

- How readily you can get an erection.
- How big it is.
- How long you can keep it up.
- How far you can push it up.
- How hard you can thrust.
- Most importantly, how many times a night you can perform.

for women:

- Are you 'ready for it' at all times?
- Are you a 'goer' (whatever that means)?
- Do you climax at precisely the same time as your lovers?
- Do you have multiple orgasms — one after another in succession?
- Do you give wonderful 'hand jobs'?
- Do you also give expert 'blow jobs'?
- Do you scream for more in bed?

Laughter, tenderness and companionship in bed are far more important than worrying about whether your performance is perfect or not.

This performance-obsessed attitude to sexuality has a definite down side, because it leaves many men and women feeling very inadequate as lovers. Although there are certain levels of sexual ability which a man or woman can reasonably expect to 'achieve' at various ages, it is far more important point to enjoy mutual warmth, tenderness, love, cuddles, companionship and laughter.

unrealistic and realistic expectations: men

When comparing myth with fact, it's helpful to look at various aspects of male sexuality, such as a man's erection, orgasm, ejaculation and expertise.

erection

MYTH. A man should be able to get a hard-on whenever he wants to and keep it going all night if necessary. Furthermore, in order for the man to qualify as really 'virile', the erection should be so vertical that the man's organ is practically touching his belly.

Most younger men can indeed reach an erection most of the time when they want to. But if they're nervous — for instance, with a new partner — it can often be very difficult. As a man gets older, he cannot expect to be able to produce an erection at a moment's notice. Although most males are potent beyond the age of 70, the number of erections which they have per day tends to diminish gradually but steadily through life.

The myth that the penis should stand up vertically during erections was debunked long ago. Dr Alfred Kinsey found that only 8–10 per cent of males 'carry the erect penis nearly vertically, more or less tightly against the belly'. He added 'the average position, calculated from all ages, is very slightly above the horizontal'.

orgasm

MYTH. Real men should be able to come time after time, with no limit to the number of orgasms they can have during a love-making session. Kinsey discovered that only males under 15 can have multiple orgasms (and only 20 per cent of them).

Women today expect foreplay and tenderness.

The vast majority of adult males cannot climax more than once in an hour, except under the most extreme sexual stimulation. Men are capable of far fewer orgasms than women, who are can reach orgasm repeatedly.

ejaculation

MYTH. Books describing sex scenes often speak of men producing vast rivers of fluid when they come.
Mr Average produces just one teaspoon of seminal fluid when he climaxes.

expertise

MYTH. Everybody is supposed to be a great lover these days; heroes in books are invariably expert at love-making — curiously enough, they rarely spend time on foreplay.
In real life, very few women will reach orgasm simply by having a penis pumping inside them. The great majority require a great deal more care and attention than that — including plenty of foreplay.

unrealistic and realistic expectations: women

Next, let's compare myth with fact as far as women are concerned. Here, it's worth looking at four different areas: enthusiasm, lubrication, orgasm and expertise.

enthusiasm

MYTH. Females are ravenous sexual creatures who are desperate to have a penis inside them at every possible moment.
Few women are as obsessed with sex as the male myth wants them to be. Unlike men, they tend not to think about sex

dozens of times every hour. Men should bear in mind that women are not always in the mood for sex. Also, a man can't expect his partner to show much enthusiasm unless he spends a good deal of time and effort in making her feel wanted, treasured, and loved.

lubrication

MYTH. Men like to think that women are always 'wet and ready'. In some novels the heroines pour out such vast quantities of love juices that it's a wonder that their lovers aren't drowned by it.

Most women's vaginas tend to be fairly dry — varying to some extent on what time of the month it is. When sexually excited, it usually takes a woman several minutes before she can produce a significant amount of lubrication. So men should bear in mind that:

To induce lubrication, spend time on foreplay.

- You shouldn't rush things.
- Spend time on foreplay and caressing her well before you try to enter.
- After the menopause, many women do become quite dry and may find it extremely hard to lubricate even when they're sexually aroused. A vaginal lubricant should help this problem; if it doesn't consult your doctor.
- A few women gush a sex fluid at the moment of orgasm from a mysterious structure that may be the equivalent of the male's prostate gland. The amount of fluid released varies, but it's often more than a man produces.

orgasm

MYTH. All real women are orgasmic from a very early age; coming the first time they have intercourse. They also have multiple orgasms from the start, and are liable to have several climaxes as soon as a man enters them.

Most women find it difficult to reach orgasm when they're young — but they do tend to find it much easier as they

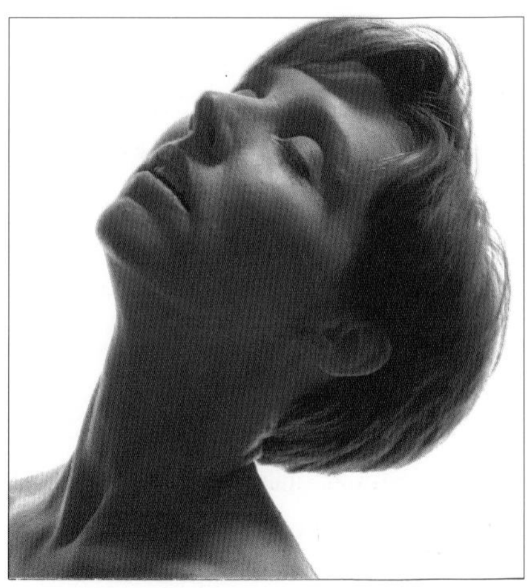

A woman should not worry about her performance.

grow older and more experienced. Women are much more likely to have multiple orgasms as they grow older, and indeed the highest incidence of multiple orgasm is in the over-45s.

expertise

MYTH. Many men think that women should be tremendously clever in bed, skilled at all sorts of erotic techniques, so able to give a man mind-blowing satisfaction all the time.

Inexperienced young women must, by definition, know next to nothing about sexual techniques. In reality, women need practice and to learn by experience before they become really skilled in such

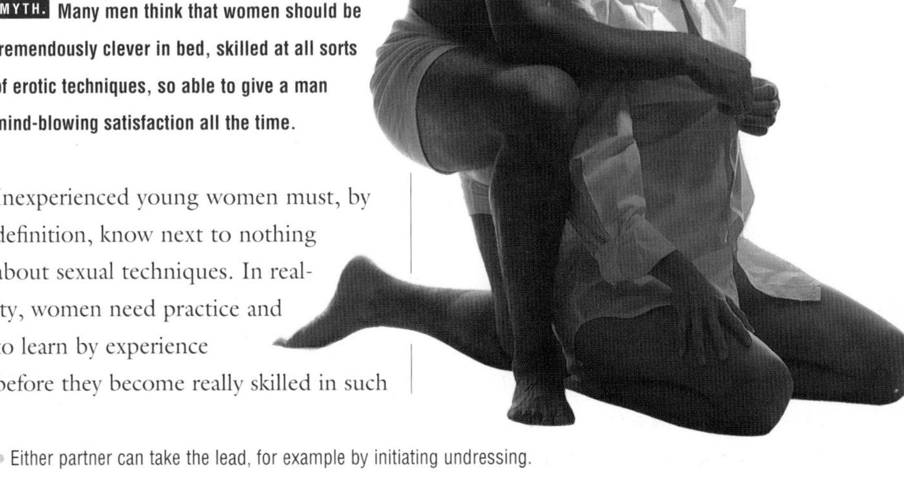

Either partner can take the lead, for example by initiating undressing.

matters as giving a good 'hand job' or 'blow job', so don't expect it of them.

For men and women in long-term, loving relationships, it's reasonable to expect your partner to learn gradually how to please you in bed.

the myth about simultaneous climax

If you relied on romantic or erotic fiction for your sex instruction, you would believe that all couples 'come' at the same time. Simultaneous orgasm is very nice when it occurs, but surveys suggest that it happens only to a minority of couples all the time. However, the more you communicate your needs to each other, the more likely a simultaneous climax will be.

When you are having intercourse, don't worry too much about simultaneous climax.

performance and trying out positions

In the last few years it has become established that a good 'performer' in bed must be able to make love in hundreds of different positions.

Some enjoyable variation in position can be very useful in keeping sex alive and enjoyable. But nobody should feel pressurized into having dozens of different positions up his or her sleeve just for the sake of it.

New positions invariably spice up a relationship.

For most couples, being able to make love in two or three different positions is usually sufficient — with perhaps a change to certain particularly comfortable ones when the woman is pregnant. Older people whose movements are limited by arthritis or rheumatism often benefit greatly by trying out a new position, and the same is true of some handicapped people. Four of the most popular, comfortable positions that don't require any strenuous acrobatics are as follows:

'Mother Superior'.

The woman simply lies on top of the man, with her legs between his. Because there is so little pressure on her abdomen, this position is recommended for pregnancy.

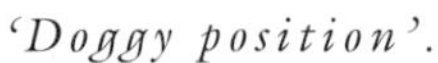

'Doggy position'.

To my surprise, this was the most popular with romantically minded women in one survey that I conducted. It's exactly as you would imagine from the (very unromantic) name: the woman kneels on all fours, and the man enters her from behind, kneeling between her calves.

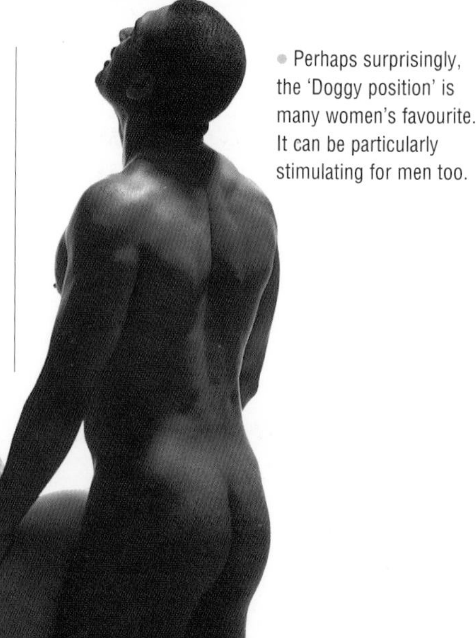

• Perhaps surprisingly, the 'Doggy position' is many women's favourite. It can be particularly stimulating for men too.

'The Chair'.

The man sits in a chair. His partner sits on his lap, facing away from him — and he enters her from below. As a variation, she can sit sideways across his lap.

'The Spoons'.

In this very comfortable position, the couple lie on their side (man behind woman) snuggled up together like two spoons in a drawer. Again, he enters her from behind. This is particularly good during pregnancy or if one of you has arthritis of the hip.

failure to achieve an erection

The main causes are:

- Tiredness
- Stress
- Worry
- Anxiety states
- Depression
- Drinking too much alcohol ('brewer's droop')
- Guilt (especially when trying to make love to somebody you shouldn't be in bed with!)
- Falling out of love/hostility to your partner

Some people think age is a major factor. The truth is that in men, the decline in potency due to advancing age is far slower than many people imagine – no less than 70 per cent of males are still potent at the age of 70.

It's important to remember that if you ever have problems with your sexual performance, there is usually a solution. Sex nearly always improves as you become more experienced at love-making. If you are not in a permanent relationship, it may just be that you and your current lover are not compatible.

2

Women and their sexual responses

Imagine a woman lying on a bed, being tenderly stroked. With skilled caresses, her lover arouses her to greater and greater heights of passion.

As her heart beats faster and faster, so does her breathing. Her vagina begins to pour out creamy love juices and her nipples become erect.

Gradually, a delicate pink flush spreads over her skin. It reaches her breasts, where the veins are suddenly more prominent. The breasts themselves have grown in size during the last few seconds — and the darkish pigmented area around each nipple is so engorged that they're almost bursting with desire. The woman's breathing becomes more urgent as the moment of climax approaches. Every muscle in her body tenses in preparation for the instant of release, the moment of orgasm...

That's how a woman reaches a climax in theory. However, the truth is that often this does not happen.

So what can be done to make sex better and more satisfying for a woman?

The sexual make-up of a woman

Good, satisfying sex is very difficult to achieve unless you know something about the sexually excitable parts of a woman's anatomy. Whether you're male or female, understanding basic female anatomy is essential for good sex.

her BREASTS

Breast size varies a great deal from woman to woman, and it's common for a woman to have one breast larger than the other. But no matter what size or shape a woman's breasts are, they still have the same erotic potential as any others. Stimulating the breasts correctly nearly always results in the recipient having tremendous sexual sensations.

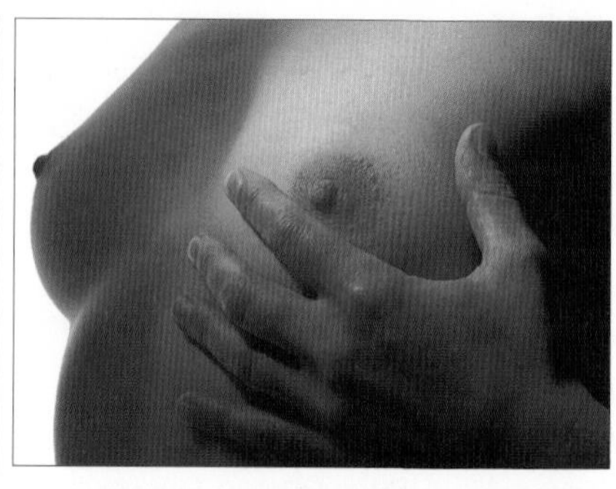

• Some women reach orgasm through nipple stimulation alone, but the majority of females cannot do this.

• The nipples have close nerve connections with the pleasure centres in the brain: they respond powerfully to stimulus.

her AREOLA

The areola is the pigmented ring around the nipple. Surprisingly few people pay enough attention to the areola when making love. It's an extremely sexually sensitive area of a woman's body, packed with delicate erotic nerve endings. Simply running a well-moistened finger-tip round the areola will pay rich dividends.

her NIPPLES

The nipple is made of erectile tissue that becomes stiff and hard under the influence of sexual stimulation, just like a man's penis does. As with the areola, a woman's nipple is positively bursting with sensitive, sensual nerve-endings, that are directly connected to the emotional and pleasure centres of her brain.

Many couples find that the most arousing nipple-stimulation technique is for the man to gently suck on it. If you are too rough with your mouth (or let your teeth catch your partner's nipple), the effect may not be at all erotic. However, some women enjoy the sensation when their nipples are lightly bitten. Ask what your lover prefers.

Parts of the Vulva

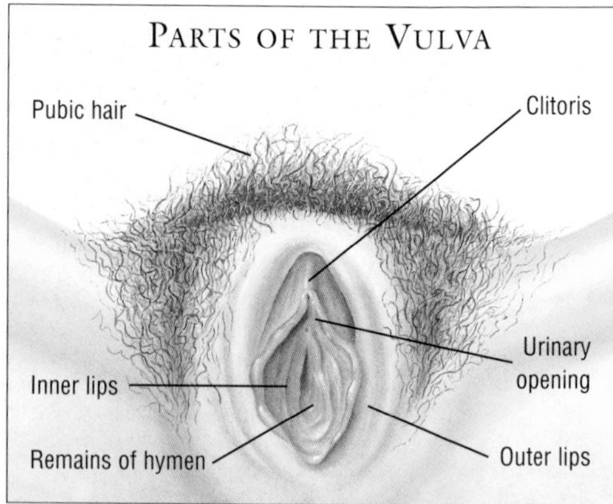

her VULVA

This refers to the outside (or visible) part of the female sex organs. Many women feel extremely embarrassed about their vulvas and think they look ugly. So it's important to be appreciative of your partner's vulva, and to reassure her that you find it attractive and exciting.

her PUBIC HAIR

The extent of pubic hair varies greatly from woman to woman. The roots are quite sensitive, so remember that gently toying with the hairs, stroking them, or giving them little tugs, is an effective way of building up sexual tension.

In order to be a skilled lover, a man must learn to stroke a woman's vulva in a way that most pleases her.

Drawing the skin gently upward over the pubic bone will increase the pleasurable tension in the labia.

her 'LIPS' *(her labia)*

The opening of a vagina is protected by two sets of lips, called 'the labia'. They are powerfully sensual parts of the body and stimulating them with the tongue or a finger is likely to give a woman very strong sexual sensations.

her CLITORIS

The clitoris is located just where the two inner lips meet at the front. To the touch, it feels a bit like a small garden pea. When a woman isn't in a state of sexual excitement, her clitoris is usually covered by a little fold of tissue called 'the hood'. But as she gets really turned on, her clitoris pushes itself outwards and becomes more visible. To orgasm, most women need clitoral stimulation.

her PUBIC BONE

You can easily locate the pubic bone by running your fingertips straight down the mid-line of pubic hair until you encounter a hard ridge just below the surface of the skin. During intercourse a good lover can try to compress his partner's clitoris, and the upper parts of the vaginal lips, between his own pubic bone and hers — thus greatly increasing the stimulation he gives her.

her URINARY OPENING

This is a tiny hole just below the clitoris. Some women like to have the urinary opening stimulated, but on no account should anything be pushed into it because you run the risk of infection or damage to the delicate tissues inside.

Make sure your fingers are clean whenever you touch this (or any other) part of the vagina.

her VAGINA

The word 'vagina' means 'sheath' — and that's exactly what it is: a sheath the size and shape to contain a man's penis.

When a woman is not sexually excited, her vagina is about 7.5cm (3in) long, but when she becomes really turned on, her vagina expands amazingly, stretching out to a length of 17cm (about 6 in) or more in some cases.

A lover should always treat his partner's vagina gently. Spend plenty of time on foreplay to ensure that enough vaginal fluid is produced to allow penetration that doesn't cause pain. Use additional lubricants if necessary.

• The vagina isn't just a pleasurable area for a penis, it's a great source of sexual excitement for a woman too.

Improving a woman's sexual response

To make sex better for his lover, a man should learn about stimulating her clitoris. The great majority of women simply cannot climax without it.

stimulating the clitoris

For most women, the clitoris is the key to their sexuality. Stroke it, caress it, lick it, suck it — in fact, do whatever she finds most pleasurable.

A man should begin any attempt at clitoral stimulation by gently caressing the area outside, gradually moving inwards and exploring with your finger-tip or tongue. If the area is a little dry and you are using a finger, try licking it first to add some moisture. Once you've found the clitoris keep the pressure firm and fast, but take care not to be rough or to scratch her with a fingernail.

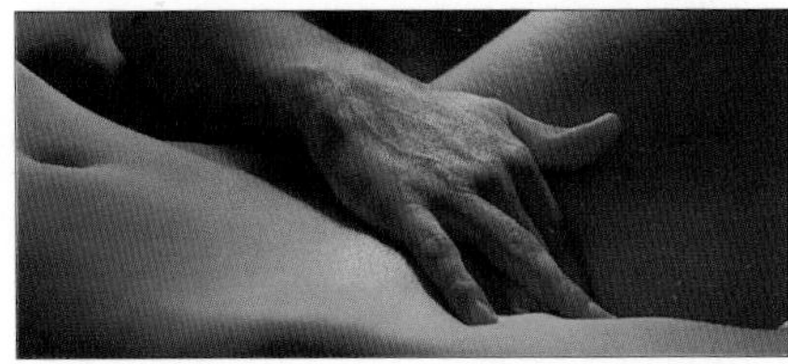

Other erogenous zones

In addition to the clitoris, a woman has many erogenous zones or areas that she likes to have caressed. If you pay special attention to your lover's erogenous zones, it will help you to turn her on. Remember though, that what one woman may find particularly exciting may not be so stimulating to another — or indeed, may even be an irritant. With experience and communication, you will discover where and how she likes to be touched. Here are some of the more important ones, ranging from the top of the body down to the feet.

behind her EARS

Most women love to be stroked, tickled and caressed behind the ears. Some become aroused when they are gently kissed here and others love to have their ears licked and their lobes sucked.

● Awakening your drowsy partner with a kiss at the base of the ear is very romantic and sexy.

the back of her NECK

The nape or back of her neck is a very sexually sensitive place. Make a point of running your lips up her spine to the point where her hair begins. Stroking this area is very erotic for many women.

her ARMPITS

These are also rather secret places so try kissing, nuzzling and licking these intimate spots. You'll probably find that the subtle feminine scents that are produced in this region of her body will be a real turn-on for you too.

her WRISTS

Don't forget to kiss or lightly stroke the inside of her wrist — a spot that is rarely touched by others, and therefore likely to be sexually sensitive.

• Kissing her neck from beneath the chin right round to the nape, whilst gently running your fingers through her hair is bound to be well received.

Don't forget to kiss her navel and ribs – areas that rate highly among the erogenous zones.

her RIBS

Ribs can frequently be quite erotic structures — especially when a woman is slim, so that they're fairly prominent. Try running your mouth along them, kissing as you go, or following the contour of a rib with the tip of your tongue or finger.

her NAVEL

The tummy button can be a surprisingly sexy part of the body; a few women can climax simply through having it stimulated. Even if this doesn't happen, just stroke it, kiss it, or run your tongue around it, this will give your partner, warm, comforting feelings.

her BUTTOCKS

The buttocks are richly supplied with sensory nerve endings. Stroking, kissing, patting and squeezing them are likely to be well received. Many couples go in for much firmer patting — in fact, smacking hard enough to produce some pain. This may not be something that you or your partner enjoy but, since many find it stimulating, it's worth considering.

It's worth caressing a woman's many erogenous zones – including her buttocks.

the insides of her THIGHS

These are sexy, ticklish spots that can be kissed, stroked and licked. Because they're on the 'final approach' to the vagina and therefore very sensuous areas, try leaving them until later in your exploration of her erogenous zones.

the backs of her KNEES

There's a theory that the nerves at the backs of the knees are connected to the nerve supply of the clitoris. However implausible this sounds, nibbling and nuzzling the backs of your loved one's knees may prove popular with her.

her TOES

Many women are turned on by what is termed a 'toe job' — in other words, sucking or gently biting one of her toes in a playful way. A few women also find that having their ankles lightly stroked with the fingers or kissed, is very erotic.

Why not try giving her a 'toe-job'?

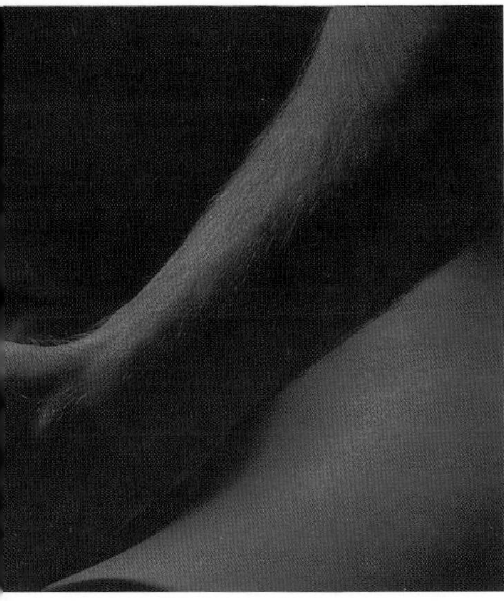

Her G-SPOT

Over recent years there has been a lot of medical argument about what exactly the G-spot is, and whether or not it exists at all. But there is no doubt that a very large number of women experience pleasurable and rather unusual sensations when this area is massaged by the tips of the fingers.

The G-spot is about 5cm (2in) or so up the front wall of the vagina. The best way to find it is to slip a moistened finger gently inside, and run it slowly up the back of the pubic bone. When you've travelled up with almost half your finger, start pressing with your finger pad against the firmness of the pubic bone. You may have to move around a little bit until you strike the spot, but your partner should tell you when you've found it. Continue rubbing there, by moving your finger backwards and forwards, and with any luck the results should be wonderful for her.

Massaging her erogenous zones

It's a really good idea to massage your partner's erogenous zones, but remember: don't rush.

I strongly recommend that you use oil when massaging. Baby oil is safest of all the types available: it's inexpensive and unlikely to cause any skin problems.

Warm the oil in your hands before you start — it's chilly when it comes out of the bottle! Having cupped a little in your palms, start by rubbing it gently into her feet. Then, using your fingertips sensuously, gradually work up her calves to the backs of her knees. Go no higher up the legs at this stage, but switch to the back of the neck, where you can spend a few minutes easing and soothing away any aches and knotted areas.

Next, work down over her shoulders and arms, pressing your fingertips gently into the muscles. Only then move to the rest of her body — perhaps starting on her ribs or shoulder blades.

Later, shift to her breasts, then work downwards over her belly to her inner thighs. By this time she will probably be desperate for you to go further.

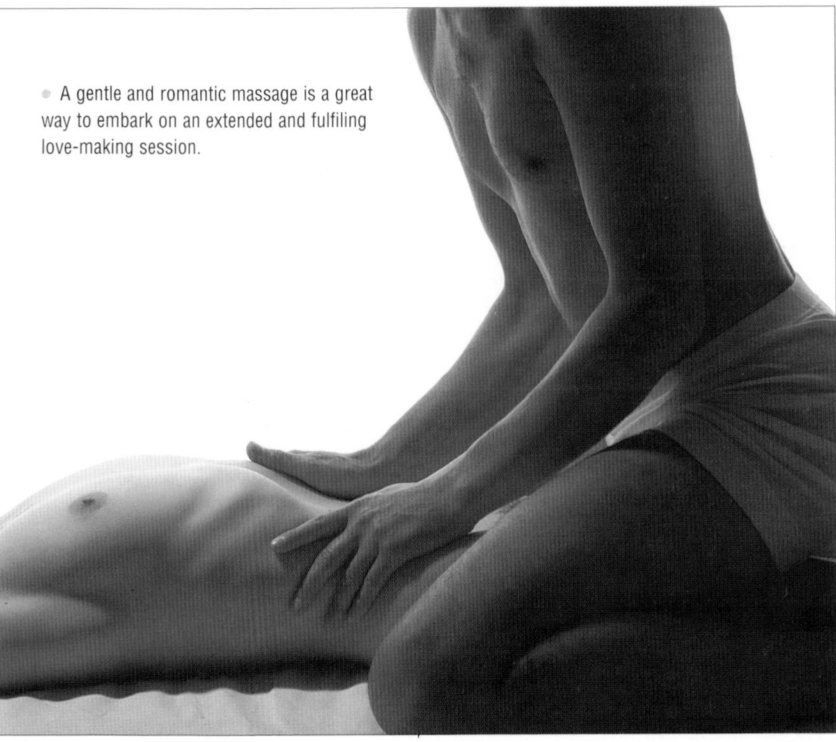

A gentle and romantic massage is a great way to embark on an extended and fulfiling love-making session.

pelvic exercises to improve a woman's sexual response

Just like any other, the muscle that surrounds the vagina can be toned up, adding to your pleasure.

There is a particular set of muscular exercises that can help to improve a woman's sexual responses. Called 'pelvic floor exercises', after the powerful muscle that surrounds the vagina, they can be done anywhere: while sitting, lying down or standing up. They're useful for any woman, whether or not she's had a baby, because they tone up the whole vaginal area, making it fitter and stronger. They give the woman the ability to grasp her man's penis while it's inside her, and make it possible for her to enjoy intercourse more. Some women who have practised the exercises over a long period say they get heightened pleasure from orgasms too.

These exercises are very easy to do.

Pelvic exercises increase the intensity of orgasm.

Tone up the front of your pelvic floor muscle first: simply imagine that you're trying very, very hard to stop yourself from passing water. Feel that muscle tighten up at the front of your pelvis and hold the contraction for 10 seconds. Then relax for 10 seconds. Repeat 10 times.

To tone up the back part of your pelvic floor, pretend that you're trying desperately to stop yourself passing a bowel motion. So, tighten up your bottom — tight, tight, tight. Hold it for 10 seconds, then release. Relax for 10 seconds, and repeat 10 times.

Do both sets of exercises twice a day — every day. It will take about six months to achieve any significant improvement, but by that time you should be noticing that your sexual response is definitely perking up.

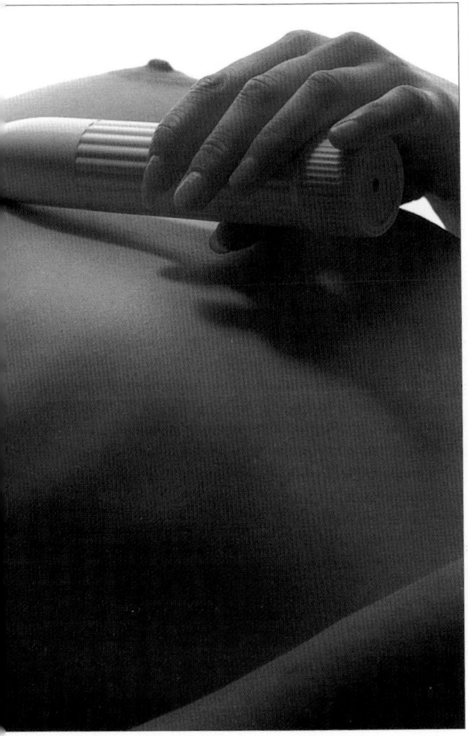

vibrators

A vibrator can be a helpful aid in love-making; many women enjoy using one, often finding it helps them to achieve orgasm, or simply to get turned on. Men shouldn't feel threatened by this, but should be prepared to use a vibrator if his partner wants him to.

How are vibrators used? Basically in whatever way a woman wants. Generally though, vibrators are used on the clitoris, and inside the vagina. Either the man, or the woman, or sometimes both partners can hold the device together. Just do whatever feels comfortable, pleasurable and right at the time.

• Vibrators are now immensely popular. They can be used on the breasts as well as on the vaginal area.

CHAPTER THREE

MEN AND THEIR SEXUAL RESPONSES

Men and their sexual responses

To achieve a good, or even better sex life, in the same way that you need to know about the sexual parts of a woman, whether you're a man or woman, you really do need some knowledge of basic male anatomy.

A man's climax is nearly always caused by stimulation of his penis – that stimulation may be provided by his lover's vagina, her hand, or some other part of her body, or his hand, or a vibrator, or whatever. Unlike women, men are not usually able to reach orgasm as a result of stimulation of another part of their body. Other factors help to bring it about – for example, psychological ones are extremely important – but the fact remains that if a man is going to reach an orgasm, it has to be through friction applied to the sensitive nerve endings in his penis. This friction will help him go through the four stages of sexual arousal: from excitement, when his penis becomes very stiff, and his heart rate, breathing rate, and pulse rate all go up; plateau stage, in which the man has achieved a high level of sexual tension, but is still in control of himself; orgasm, the point at which the man just has to let go (or rather come); and resolution, the period in which everything calms down and returns to normal.

The sexual structure of men is much simpler to understand than that of women – partly because most of the sexual equipment is on the outside. Let's consider the parts one by one.

his PENIS

Most men think about (and worry about) their penises throughout their lives.

In its non-erect (limp or flaccid) state this fleshy organ is about 5–10cm (2–4in) long. Most of the outside of the penis is covered with soft skin that is very sensitive and packed with more sexual nerve endings than anywhere else in the male body. Whatever you do to that soft skin (within reason), from stroking it with your fingertips to touching it up with your tongue, will be very pleasant for your man and may indeed induce

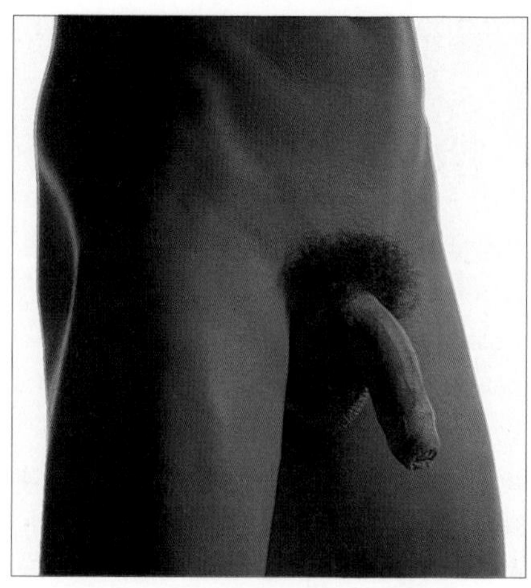

• Mental or physical stimulation make blood enter.

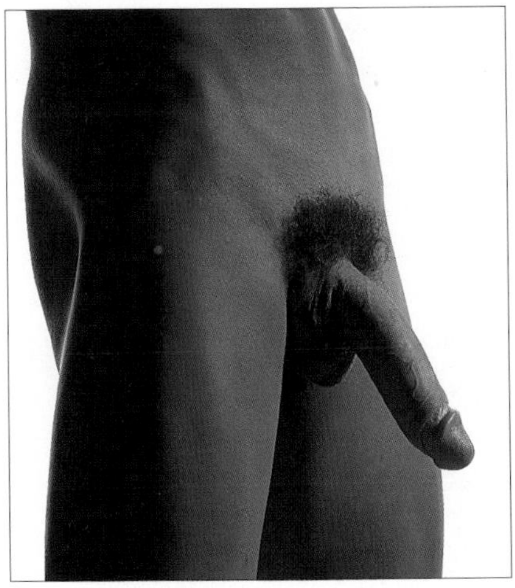

Like filling a hosepipe, the penis then expands.

orgasm. The inside of the penis is made up of three cavities which can fill up with blood during sexual excitement. It's this filling-up process (sometimes called 'tumescence') which makes the penis stiffen into erection.

The tip of the penis is amazingly sensitive too. In shape and colour, it's rather like a plum, and its medical name is the 'glans'. Its surface, which has a pleasant velvety feel to it, is what nuzzles

The internal pressure helps it toward full erection.

up against the top end of the vagina during intercourse.

Another important part of the penis is the foreskin, or prepuce. When a man has an erection, his foreskin should roll right back, so that the glans is completely uncovered. In some men this does not happen, even during sexual intercourse. This is unhygienic as well as being unsatisfying sexually. If your prepuce won't go back, you should have it removed surgically — an operation known as circumcision.

worries about penis size

There are very few men who haven't at some time taken a tape measure and surreptitiously measured themselves – and then worried about whether they're big enough. Indeed, some men go through life utterly convinced that their penises are too small. The facts about penis size:

- Most penises are much the same size erect as they are when limp.
- A man with a penis on the small side will as a rule achieve something like a 100 per cent increase in length during erection, whereas a man whose limp penis is large will often achieve only a 70 per cent increase in length when he becomes erect.
- The majority of men measure between 15cm (about 6in) and 18cm (around 7in) long when they are sexually aroused.
- The penises of all races are much the same length when erect.
- Size most definitely has no relationship to potency: a man can have a huge organ and be (a) impotent; (b) a lousy lover.

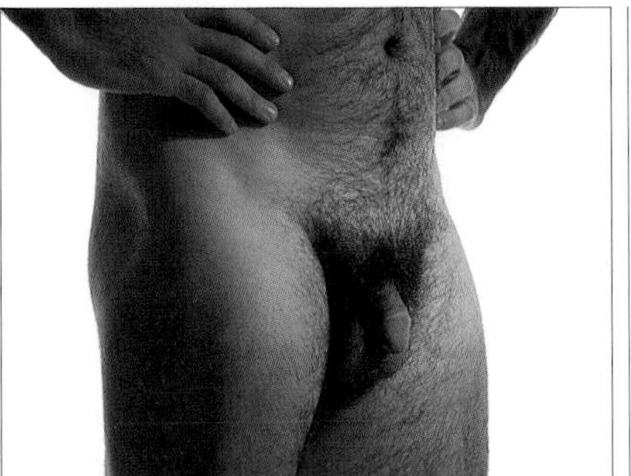

This penis looks rather small, but that is mainly because its owner is feeling cold.

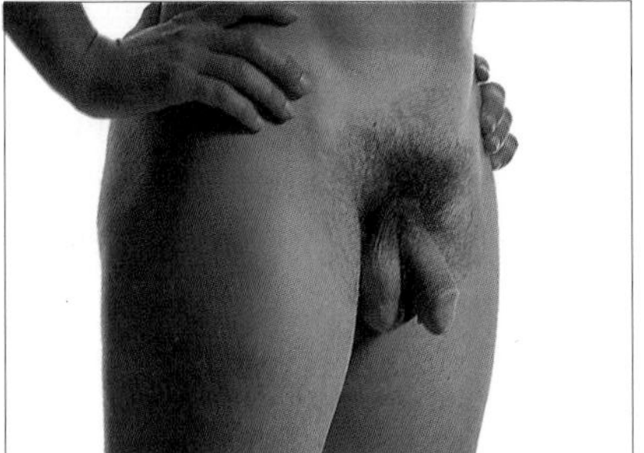

This largish penis would probably be erroneously regarded by it's owner as small.

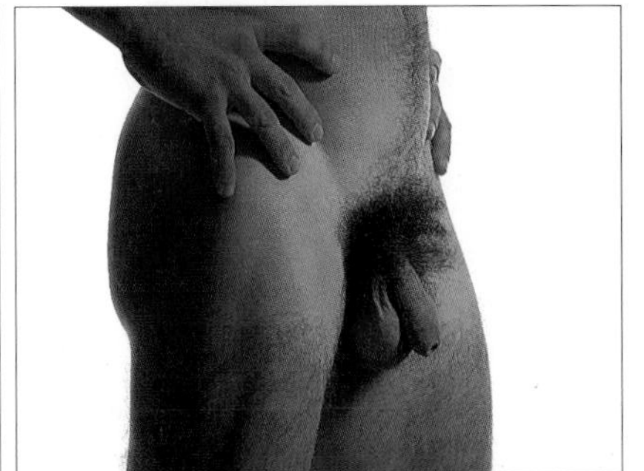

This man's penis is on the large size when non-erect, but will be average size when he's excited.

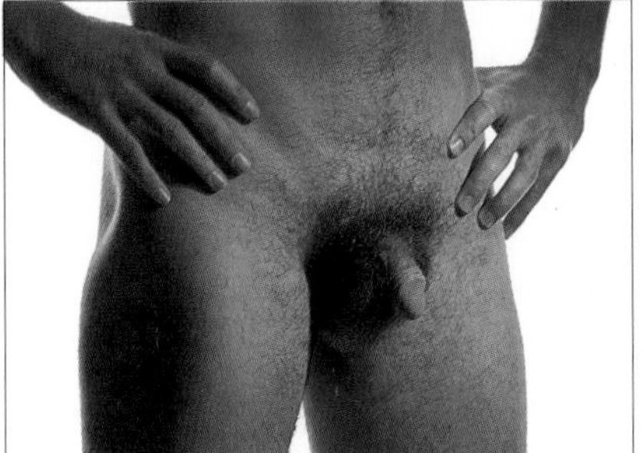

This circumcised penis looks tiny, but is quite capable of lengthening to 15cm (6in) or more.

If you feel inadequate where size is concerned, bear in mind that many women feel frightened or revolted by the idea of having a very big penis thrust inside them.

his TESTICLES

A man's testicles (his balls) are his two sex glands, which are very tender and should be handled gently. They're located just beneath his penis, inside the little pouch of skin called the scrotum. They have two functions:

- To produce male sex hormones, which flow round the bloodstream and give the man his male sex characteristics, such as hairiness, muscularity, a deep voice, aggression, and sexual desire.
- To produce the sperms that swim in seminal fluid.

The average testicle weighs about 12gm which is slightly under half an ounce – less weighty than most people would think. It's roughly oval-shaped and is about 5cm (around 2in) in length and 2.5cm (about 1in) across. It's quite common for one testicle to be slightly larger than the other, this is nothing at all to worry about. Also, one normally hangs lower than the other. Most men are born with two testicles, but a few, perfectly healthy, men have three or one.

Men like having their testicles carefully handled. They find this sexually exciting – but no amount of stroking or fondling the testicles can by itself cause an orgasm. I must stress that these two glands are very tender, so do not squeeze them hard, or accidentally hit them with your knee or elbow.

Men and sexual arousal

An erection is the man's equivalent of the lubrication that begins in a woman's vagina, and just like a woman, there are plenty of ways that men can be aroused.

Though the penis is the most important, don't neglect your lover's other erogenous zones.

Any women in pursuit of good sex should know what turns men on and how to help this happen. An erection is the first obvious physical sign of sexual arousal in a man. An erection happens because the tubes that normally carry the blood out of the three cylinders in the penis close, trapping the blood inside. These mysterious alterations in blood flow initially occur because of changes in the emotional centres of the man's brain when he starts to think about making love – and especially if his partner starts talking to him about sex. These changes send nerve impulses down his spinal cord to the 'sex nerves' in his pelvis, which supply his penis.

Helping a man to get and keep an erection is generally quite easy if you do one or all of the following:

- Stroke, fondle and rub his penis with your fingers.
- Suck his penis — often the most effective erection-inducer of all.
- Say sexy things to him — erotic words in his ear can be a powerful stimulant to erection.

An imaginative woman can use her breasts as well as her hands, tongue and lips, to caress and arouse her lover. There are plenty of other erogenous zones in the male body other than the penis, and couples who neglect these in their love-making are definitely missing out. In the next section we look at some of the main erogenous zones for men.

Oral sex is a loving and effective way of helping a man to achieve a full erection.

Erogenous zones in men

Although it's not usually difficult to turn a man on simply by going directly for his penis and fondling it, he'll get a lot more pleasure if you spend some time on his erogenous zones first.

his HAIR

Most men like having their hair ruffled and stroked. Obviously this does not apply if your man wears a wig or toupee. Bald men often like having the top of the scalp stroked and kissed.

under his JAW

There is a quite sexually sensitive area under the jaw, just on either side of the Adam's apple. Nuzzling and kissing here usually produces good results.

his EARS

Most men's ears are just as sensitive as women's – in fact, this is one of the erogenous zones that the sexes share. Kissing, licking and nuzzling a man's ears are likely to turn him on, though some men hate it and find it too ticklish.

his BACK MUSCLES

Nearly all men love having their back muscles stroked, massaged and gently prodded.

Don't forget that your lover will almost certainly appreciate it if you lick and suck his earlobes.

Sitting astride him, use your outspread fingers to massage his bottom – a very sensual area of his body.

his NIPPLES

Few people realize that, like the corresponding area in women, the male nipple and surrounding areola are sensitive. Stroking, kissing, gently pinching or nipping can often turn on a man.

his BOTTOM

The buttocks and the anus are heavily supplied with sensual nerve endings. However, if you decide to stroke your lover around the anal area, make sure you wash your hands before touching anything else or you may risk infection.

his FEET

Feet are quite sexy parts of the body. A 'toe job' simply means taking your man's big toe or any other one you fancy in your mouth, and making agreeable up-and-down sucking movements.

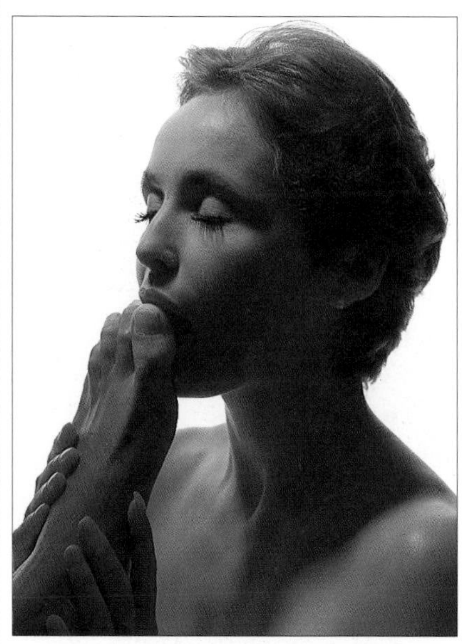

Why not pour a few drops of champagne over his big toe – and enjoy sucking it!

Massaging his erogenous zones

Having a massage is nearly always a pleasurable experience, but having your erogenous zones sensually massaged by a lover is simply wonderful. Before you start, the man should lie naked and face down on the bed.

Men really love having their erogenous zones massaged. To begin, lubricate your hands with a little baby oil or talcum powder, which will make the palms and fingertips slide over the skin. Start by kneading his shoulders and upper back. Work slowly down his spine, prodding gently in between the bones. When you get to his bottom, use your outspread hands to stroke his buttocks lovingly. Remember too that many men have a considerable enthusiasm for a few gentle smacks in this area.

Next, work up and down the insides of his thighs, and the back of his calves. Only then should you turn him over. You can prolong the fun a little longer by stroking his nipples and massaging the muscles of his belly before finally moving down to his, by now, eager sex organs.

• Ask your partner what he or she most wants in bed – but do experiment as well.

what men wish women knew

Ideally, you should ask your partner what he/she wants in bed but many people find this difficult. Try to communicate with your partner – it really will pay dividends for your relationship. Here are some of the things that most men relish in bed.

1 *rude talk*

While there are a few men who insist on making love in perfect silence, most of them find it really exciting when a woman decides to 'talk dirty'.

2 *enthusiasm*

Some women and men still approach love-making in a half-hearted fashion, perhaps with one eye on the clock or on the TV. An enthusiastic approach to sex should spark an equal response in your partner.

3 *laughter*

Keeping a sense of humour can be more valuable than a hundred orgasms. If you can give your man a bit of a giggle between the sheets, you'll be doing yourselves a lot of good. Some couples find that if sex is always a serious matter, stress can creep in, with adverse affects on performance and the relationship.

4 *willingness to experiment*

A little innovation can greatly improve your sex. Different positions can make love-making less routine.

Don't be afraid to let yourself go and scream while you are engaged in passionate love-making.

5 *handling and massage*

Men invariably love their genitals being touched. Keep a bottle of baby oil handy so that you can rub it lingeringly into all the secret bits of his body whenever the mood dictates.

6 *dressing for sex*

For many people seeing their partner dressed in certain clothes is really exciting, and it doesn't necessarily have to be 'kinky' gear either. Also, try making love semi-nude; very erotic for some people.

7 *being willing to strip*

Stripping can be an exciting part of foreplay, and most men find it very stimulating to watch a woman gradually take off her clothes.

coming too soon

In many relationships (particularly young couples') the man tends to be explosively triggered. In other words, he 'goes off' a little too soon. In extreme cases, this is referred to as 'premature ejaculation'. There are certain things that a couple can do to make the man capable of lasting longer and postponing his orgasm:

- Make a pact that the man will tell the woman by some signal when he thinks orgasm is near.
- From that moment, she should immediately stop wriggling, thrusting and saying or doing sexy things until he's calmer.
- When he feels orgasm getting quite

near, the man should divert his mind by thinking about something un-sexy

- Additionally, he may be able to distract himself physically by clenching his teeth together hard, or by pinching or even biting himself.
- Changing rhythm or simply pausing for a while may help.

Deciding where 'coming a bit too soon' becomes full-blown premature ejaculation, isn't really relevant. Clearly, if a man climaxes before even getting inside his partner, he has severe PE. Some people would say that a man who can't prolong intercourse beyond five minutes has mild PE.

If the simple measures outlined above haven't helped you delay the male climax very much, it's probably time to seek professional help. An excellent self-help treatment for this kind of problem has been available for some years: a special grip which a therapist can easily teach a couple. When this grip is applied to the penis, it will immediately take away the desire to ejaculate.

The grip which cures 'PE' must be taught precisely by an expert; if it's wrong it won't work!

CHAPTER FOUR

4

OVERCOMING SEXUAL INHIBITIONS

Overcoming sexual inhibitions

We all have a number of inhibitions. An inhibition is a block to certain thoughts or behaviour set up by our unconscious – and some are sexual.

Many people have sexual inhibitions. This isn't really surprising because everyone has inhibitions of some kind. Psychologists will tell you that human beings comprise a mass of inhibitions — some are sexual, but many are not.

For instance, most of us grow up with inhibitions or fear about getting ourselves burned through going too near a fire. We've developed that particular inhibition for two main reasons:

- In early childhood, our parents or elders 'inhibited' us from getting too close to the flames by pulling us away or telling us very firmly that messing around with fire was dangerous.
- Second, if we were unwise enough to go near a fire we rapidly discovered that what we had been warned against was true — we did indeed get burned. This provided us with another powerful inhibition against playing with fire.

Now let's turn to sexual inhibitions. Virtually everybody in Western society is still brought up by their parents to regard their sex organs as being taboo. Even in the most liberated of households, there is parental pressure on children to hide their sex organs from strangers, and not to flaunt them in public.

In less liberal-minded homes, the inhibitions that parents instill can be very much greater. A parent that screams at a child (or threatens her with violence) because she has been touching herself, gives a frightening signal that will imprint itself on her mind for life. She will always retain something of a feeling that sex must be pretty dreadful — because if you touch yourself it follows that you get hit or shouted at.

Although most Western families aren't so repressive today, many children are still taught at an early age that the lower parts of the human body are 'rude' or 'dirty'.

The human sex organs are arranged so that they're mixed up with the organs of excretion. It's a pity that we make love with the parts that we urinate with, for this has given vast numbers of men and women terrible hang-ups.

Strangely, urine is not actually dirty. Many people find this hard to believe, but it's absolutely true. Urine may not be the pleasantest liquid in the world, but it is normally germ-free. However, it is quite true that people's bottoms (that is, their rectums) are dirty, because bowel motions contain large amounts of germs. Some of these germs can be dangerous to health.

You need to cast off your inhibitions if you want to enjoy your relationship to the full.

some inhibitions are good; some are bad

Sex is a very pleasurable and powerful driving force in most people: if we had no inhibitions whatever, it's possible we would all be having intercourse with any personable stranger who happened along.

Humans need some sexual inhibitions to prevent the spread of disease and maintain relationships, but it's a pity we have quite so many because they can clutter up people's love lives and make them deeply unhappy.

ALCOHOL *and* INHIBITIONS

Millions of people all over the world use alcohol to overcome their inhibitions — sexual and otherwise. The main reason alcohol works so effectively is because it suppresses the front part of the brain, where our inhibitions are controlled.

That is why small doses of alcohol are good for loosening up people who might otherwise have been overly reserved or unforthcoming.

Small doses of alcohol can also aid your sex life a little. One or two modest-sized drinks can help you discard your more constricting inhibitions, so that you have a good time in bed with your partner.

On the other hand, larger doses of alcohol can have a devastating effect on people's sexual inhibitions. Under the influence of alcohol, previously respectable people can do crazy things — like seduce a friend's partner or have a passionate holiday romance with a stranger. Excessive alcohol can also have a damaging effect on men, who find that they become impotent — that is, they fail to get an erection — afflicted with the aptly named 'brewer's droop'.

Other DRUGS *and* INHIBITIONS

A number of the illegal substances such as Ecstasy (or 'E'), are popular mainly because they help to get rid of inhibitions and — in some cases — increase the chance of sexual 'scoring' as a consequence.

This may sound good, but the trouble with virtually every drug — including both Ecstasy and alcohol — is that before long, you start to need bigger doses to get the same liberating effect. Furthermore, every drug that reduces the inhibitions can have very serious side-effects.

Both men and women can be affected by inhibitions which detract from their enjoyment of sex.

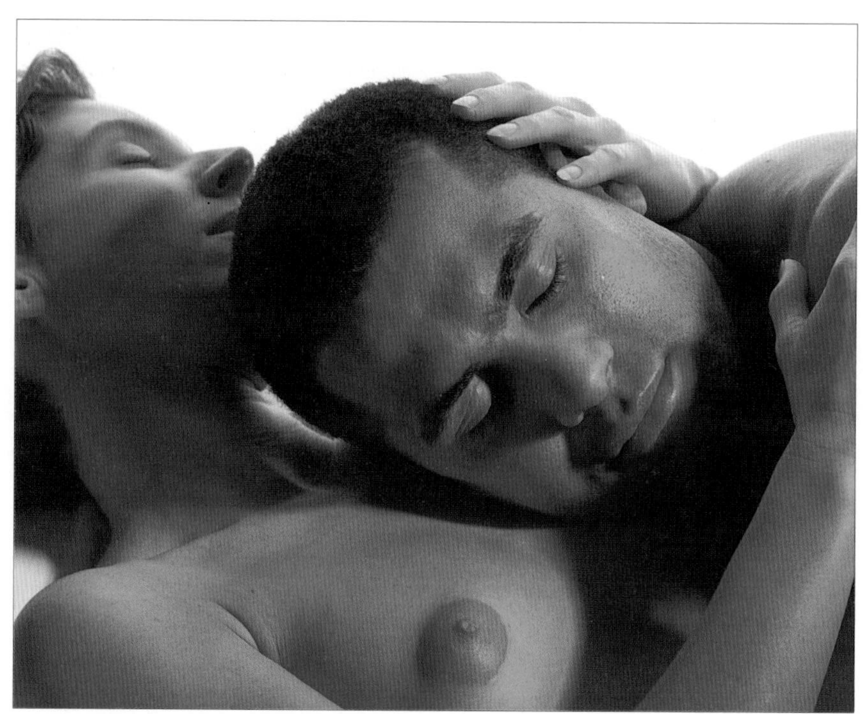

Once inhibitions have been overcome, sex can be much more fulfiling for both partners.

inhibitions about STRIPPING

Many people are very inhibited about taking off their clothes in front of someone else, and there are a number of women and men whose partners have never seen them naked.

Partly this inhibition is due to early childhood conditioning. Another factor is that many people are embarrassed about defects in their bodies — or what they think are imperfections. A lot of men are reluctant to be seen naked because they have a bit of paunch; many women are terrified of being seen nude because they think their breasts are saggy, or because they have spots on their bottoms (a very common condition).

Reluctance to strip off can damage your sex life — particularly if your inhibition starts to irritate your partner. To put things right, you have to confront the problem in a mutually supportive way.

inhibitions about KEEPING THE LIGHT ON

Quite a few people won't make love if the light is on. This can be very off-putting for a partner who wants to have the benefit of seeing his/her loved one's face and body during intercourse.

The origins of this inhibition are the same as those about stripping and if you want to defeat the problem, you have to confront it.

inhibitions about TOUCHING SEX ORGANS

These inhibitions are surprisingly common. For instance, quite a few men have great difficulty in touching their partner's vagina or clitoris. Clearly, men who suffer from this hang-up are not going to be successful lovers.

These men have often been brought up with the irrational idea that women and their sex organs are 'dirty' or to be feared. This may simply be a fear of the unknown that will disappear with practice.

inhibitions about NAMING SEX ORGANS

Good sex largely depends on men and women being able to talk to their lovers about their likes and dislikes. However, many couples find it difficult to communicate during love-making because they have no way of telling each other what they want.

Often, the reason is that they can't say the words that describe the sex organs. Some have difficulty saying the words that describe the 'naughty bits'. This stems from the repressive attitudes of a generation ago, when words like 'penis', 'vagina' and 'clitoris' were never printed, so most people grew up with only a limited knowledge of sex words.

inhibitions about MASTURBATION

It's possible that more people have hang-ups about masturbation than any other sexual topic. Many men and women feel enormous guilt about wanking — the slang term for masturbation.

This is not surprising, because it's not that long since adults told youngsters that it would damage their eyes or make hair grow on their palms. For much of this century, masturbation was

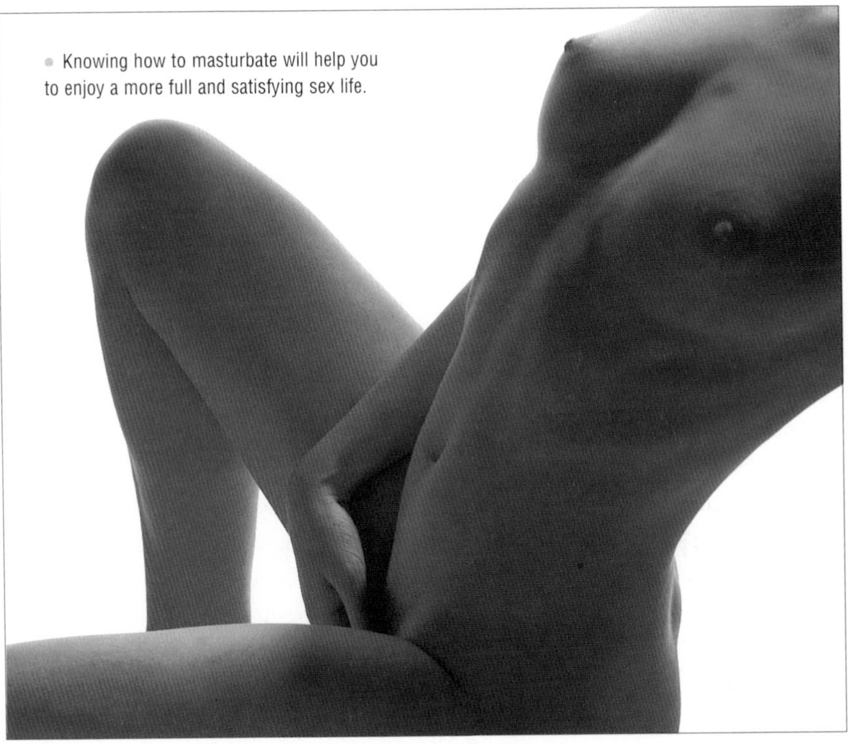

Knowing how to masturbate will help you to enjoy a more full and satisfying sex life.

regarded as 'the secret vice', or 'self-abuse'. Happily, the following is now common knowledge:

- Masturbation (male or female) isn't dangerous — it's totally harmless, and can in fact improve a couple's sex life.
- The vast majority of men and women have enjoyed masturbating — or touching themselves — at some time.
- Many men and women masturbate throughout their lives.
- Masturbation frequently forms part of the love play between couples.
- Using masturbation with your lover in this way can often be liberating for both of you.

inhibitions about ORAL SEX

Oral sex doesn't appeal to everyone — and if a couple don't want to practise it, there's obviously no reason why they should.

However, an increasing amount of men and women do enjoy oral caresses. Generally inhibitions about oral sex are centred around receiving or giving it.

inhibitions about RECEIVING IT

A man may feel inhibited about receiving oral sex from a woman because he genuinely fears that she will bite his penis. A woman may fear receiving oral sex because she may think that she doesn't smell very nice or look very nice 'down below'.

Both sexes may be worried about receiving oral sex because they fear they might fart near their lover's face — an embarrassing prospect indeed!

inhibitions about GIVING IT

Women may be wary of giving oral sex because they're afraid that the penis might choke them, or because they dislike the appearance and taste of seminal fluid. Men may dislike giving oral sex because they have fears about the vagina, or can't cope with its exotic smell and taste.

If one of a couple does have any of these worries, then it's important that the two of them should talk things through and discuss how they feel about it.

how inhibitions CHANGE WITH AGE

Young people often assume that their elders are sexually inhibited. This is nonsense as a rule. (Of course, the social permissiveness or otherwise of the era in which someone was brought up, will have a bearing on how inhibited they are.) In general, people do not become more sexually inhibited as they grow older. In fact, the reverse is often true. This is particularly true of women, who often find it difficult to lie back and 'let go' when they're teenagers. But by their middle years, they are often having orgasms frequently. It's worth reminding yourself that inhibitions don't have to stay with you for life and it's quite possible to leave them behind you.

overcoming inhibitions

Maybe your inhibition is actually right for you, or maybe it isn't. You need to decide this for yourself.

Communication is nearly always the best starting point when trying to resolve a sexual problem. In general, you should begin by talking openly with your partner. It may also help if you discuss things with good friends or relatives whom you trust.

You may that you want to consult a professional: for example, a doctor, a nurse, a psychologist, a marriage guidance or youth counsellor, or a sex therapist. Remember it's more than likely that they've already helped others overcome similar inhibitions.

Whatever you do, begin gradually! In most cases it's best to tackle your sexual inhibitions very slowly — if possible take some months to break the problem down into smaller compartments.

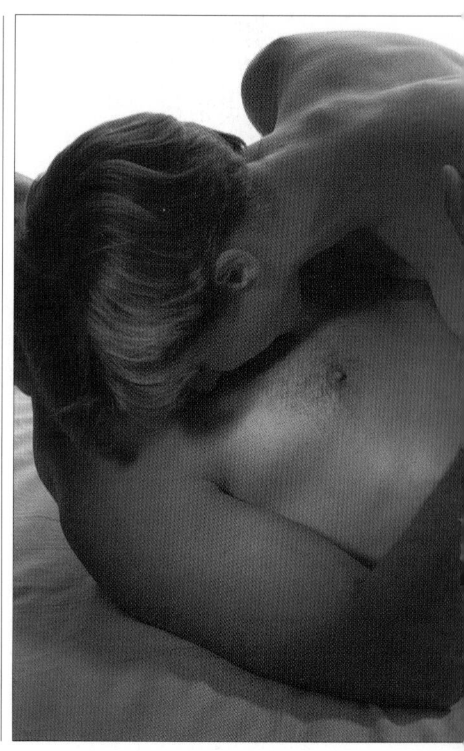

As people gain more maturity and experience they tend to become far less inhibited in bed.

HIV & AIDS

Most doctors believe that AIDS (Acquired Immune Deficiency Syndrome) is caused by HIV (Human Immunodeficiency Virus). Someone who has been infected with HIV will remain well for some years, but they will probably be infectious, and eventually develop AIDS. When HIV gets into the bloodstream, it begins to attack the cells which help prevent other diseases taking hold. If AIDS develops, the sufferer is overwhelmed by infections, skin tumours and dementia. As yet there is no cure or vaccine against HIV. There are three main ways that HIV can be transmitted: from mother to unborn child; by drug users sharing needles; by people having unprotected penetrative sex (vaginal, or especially, anal). HIV is present in an infected person's body fluids (including tears), and it can be passed on through blood, semen and vaginal fluid. With such a terrible disease claiming increasing numbers of victims worldwide, the importance of the proper use of a condom is obvious (see pages 77-81), whether for a man or woman.

CHAPTER FIVE

Sexual techniques

Sex shouldn't just be a mechanical business. Books about human sexuality can give the impression that love-making is a technical skill that you learn like fretwork or basketweaving. Whilst it's vital to know about the mechanics of sex, techniques should be seen as the building blocks to a total experience.

It may come as a surprise that I should begin with what many people regard as the most basic of all sexual techniques: kissing. Few of us explore the possibilities for pleasure that it affords. Kissing is one of the cornerstones of good sex, offering many possibilities for mutual pleasure. Here are some tips for improving your kissing technique and therefore your relationship.

french kisses

There are no rules at all about whether the man or the woman should put their tongue inside the mouth of the person they're kissing. It depends on what gives most pleasure and how the kiss develops. If you detect any feeling of revulsion or 'pulling back' in your partner, withdraw your tongue. You may have misjudged his or her enthusiasm.

Skilled French kissing is quite an art: don't confine yourself to 'sticking your tongue down the throat'. Try to explore all of your partner's mouth — provided that he or she responds well.

1 kiss as often as you can.

Many women, and a few men, complain that their partners don't kiss them enough. 'He only wants one thing, and he can't be bothered to kiss me before he does it' is a frequent cry. Such complaints are extremely common after a relationship has been going for a long time.

2 kiss him/her all over.

Don't just confine yourself to the lips — go for all the nooks and crannies of the body as well: neck, breasts, nipples, armpits, navel, pubes, wherever.

Every secret place in the body is fair game except the anus, which is a definite health hazard for the person doing the kissing. Anal kissing, known as anilingus or 'rimming', usually involves running your tongue around your partner's anus and is an activity that must now be regarded as unsafe.

For an erotic turn-on with a difference, try French kissing upside-down for a change!

3 variants to develop the art of French kissing.

- Put your tongue into the space between his/her teeth and cheeks.
- Raise the tip of your tongue so that it strokes your lover's palate.
- Turn your head so that it's upside-down to your partner's head. Then ease your tongue in so that the top surfaces of the two tongues can stroke each other — a quite unusual sensation.

raising the question of condoms

Some couples don't use condoms because they're embarrassed about raising the issue. Today, from a health point of view, a condom should always be used in any new relationship. The notion of 'safer sex' should offend nobody who's got any sense. Both the male and female condom can easily be accommodated in a wallet, purse or pocket.

Assuming one of you is carrying condoms, you've still got to deal with saying that you want to use one. If possible, it's much easier if you have already discussed the topic of AIDS (see page 73), safer sex and condoms, well before the moment when passion takes over and rational thought might be abandoned.

the FEMALE CONDOM

No extensive research has yet been done to show how effective the female condom is for preventing pregnancy or protecting against sexually transmitted diseases. However, it does offer some protection against AIDS. It also gives the woman some degree of autonomy over the question of protection.

Shaped like a small bin-liner, it's made of clear polyurethane. Like the condom for men, it can only be used once. The woman (or her man) slips it into her vagina before intercourse (an advantage over the male condom because it can be inserted in advance).

the MALE CONDOM

Putting it On

Many people don't know how to use a condom. This is very risky because if you put in on incorrectly, you may end up with an unwanted pregnancy or infection, or both. If you haven't worn a condom before, it will help if you practise handling one in private before you need to use one for real.

• Having pressed the air out of the teat at the end, put the condom over the tip of the erect penis.

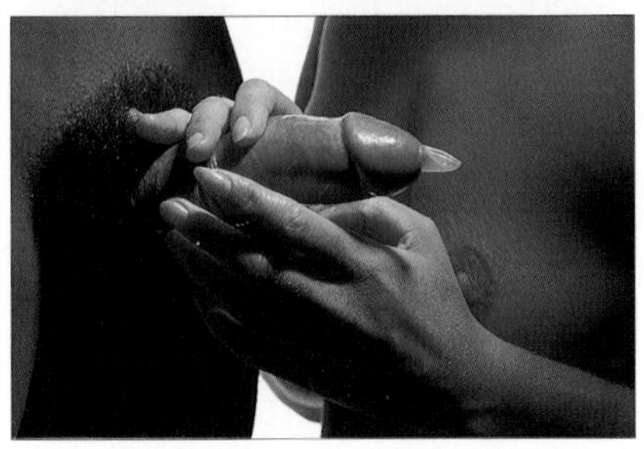

• Continue rolling the condom on. If the erection begins to weaken, just give the penis a swift rub!

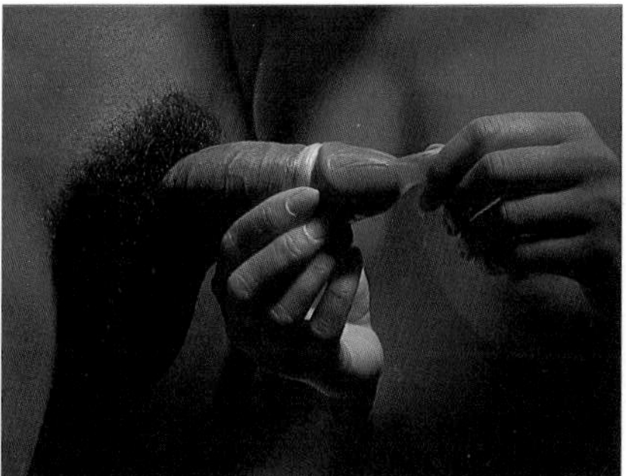

Gently start unrolling it on to the penis, taking care not to tear it with your fingernails or jewellry.

Finally, roll the condom securely to the very base of the erect penis before entering the vagina.

Here's a step-by-step guide to putting on a condom (always a new one, which hasn't passed its expiry date).

1 Make sure that you don't tear it with fingernails or jewellry.

2 Take it out of its packet. Without unrolling it, put it in an accessible place.

3 Do not make the common mistake of blowing it up to see if there are any holes in it – this could weaken it.

4 When you both want to start intercourse — assuming you have an erection — lie on your back and pick up the condom.

5 Use your finger and thumb to press the air out of the little teat at the end of the condom to make room for the semen.

6 Roll it carefully onto the erect penis with your fingers.

7 Carry on lovemaking.

It is important not to submit to the temptation to postpone putting on a condom. Many couples let the penis enter the vagina for a while, then withdraw and put on the condom for the final thrusts. This is dangerous, because a man can impregnate a woman with seminal fluid before his orgasm.

Taking it off

Avoid spillage when removing a condom. If the man just pulls his penis out some time after he's reached his climax, the sheath may come off, partly or completely. It may even be left inside his lover.

Soon after orgasm, while he's still partially erect, the man should hold the condom at the base of the penis with two fingers while he gently withdraws from the vagina.

If you don't do this fairly soon after you come, there's a danger that sperm will leak out as your penis shrinks inside the condom. Once you're out of the vagina, take the sheath off, tie a knot in it, and dispose of it thoughtfully.

There will now be sperm on your penis and possibly on your fingers — so don't put either anywhere near the woman's vagina till you've had a wash.

problems of condom technique

People have two main complaints when using condoms:

- 'My man can't use one.' This probably means that he loses his erection when he tries to put a condom on. The solution is for the woman to put it on while rubbing his penis, and saying encouragingly sexy things.

- The condom bursts or slips off. Condoms do sometimes burst. It's also quite common for them to come off accidentally. The condom should not slip off if you follow the step-by-step guide on page 79.

If, after intercourse, you find that a condom has burst, you should consider emergency contraception. If given within 72 hours after intercourse, the post-coital ('morning after') pill is 96–99 per cent effective in preventing pregnancy. Alternatively, the IUD (coil) can be inserted within five days, with a success rate of nearly 100 per cent. A table of various contraceptive methods, with a brief description of how they work and their advantages and disadvantages, is given on page 94.

Orgasm

Inexperienced lovers tend to have orgasms in a most chaotic fashion. The more sexually experienced a couple are the more control they should be able to exercise over their climaxes — especially if they've been together for some time.

But inevitably mistakes will happen, and nobody should be worried if occasionally the man can't help climaxing too soon — or the woman simply can't reach a climax at all.

Unfortunately, there are many men who don't care whether they reach orgasm too soon or whether she climaxes at all. This is selfish behaviour.

So what constitutes good behaviour orgasm-wise? Let's look at men and women separately.

men

A man should try to hold on for a reasonable time before he has his climax. Most women want to increase duration of foreplay and intercourse. Some surveys suggest that the average woman prefers over half an hour of intercourse if possible.

Try to ensure that your partner has at least one climax — before or after yours. Even if you're exhausted after coming, you should make the effort if she's not satisfied.

women

The best thing you can do climax-wise is simply let the man know what you want, when you want it. Tell him about whatever is starting to take your fancy.

Most important, try to let the man

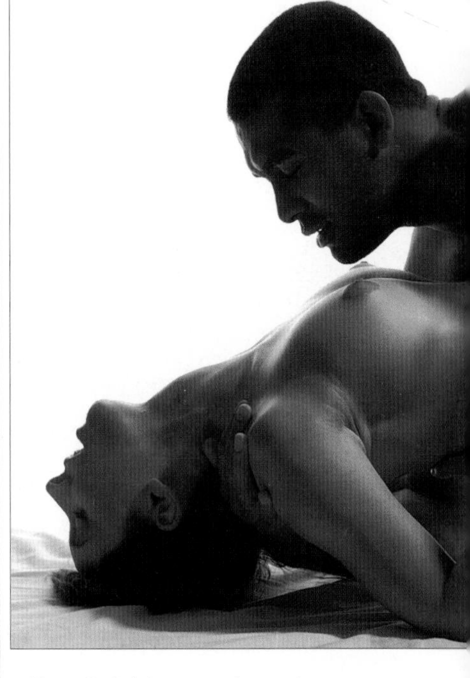

• Always try to let your man know when you are about to come by giving some visible or audible sign.

know when you're getting near to, and when you actually reach, orgasm. Many men have difficulty in discerning how excited their partners are. If you're not the type who screams wildly when you come, a man may be unable to tell whether you've got there or not.

Finally, is it OK for you to masturbate to help you climax? Certainly: though some men can't cope with the sight of a woman doing this, most of them find it a real turn-on.

Oral Sex

People tend to have very strong feelings about oral sex. Some are disgusted by it — but a very large number of couples derive a great deal of pleasure, fun and satisfaction from it.

Cunnilingus, when expertly done, can give women the most intense and powerful stimulation.

One important point: you should not perform oral sex if you've got a cold, a sore throat or indeed any kind of infection of the mouth or nose. There are occasions when a mouth infection can be transferred to the sex organs. Most importantly, a cold sore on the lip could give your lover genital herpes.

cunnilingus

Cunnilingus is oral sex given by a man to a woman or a woman to a woman.

Don't be shy about offering your partner cunnilingus: she'll probably be very grateful. If she's not too keen, she can just move your head gently away.

Should you say you're going to do it? Some men like to enquire but it's doubtful this is strictly necessary. It may be simpler just to get on with it.

However, do not lunge at your partner's vulva, especially if it's the first time you have done this together. Approach her vulva very gradually, moving your lips slowly from her breasts, down over her abdomen, and then through her pubic hair. Once you've started kissing her vulva, do not use your teeth at all — it's an extremely sensitive area. Cunnilingus should be carried out only with the tongue and lips.

Some women become very sensitive in their clitoris after they've come once or twice, so if your partner suddenly pushes you away from her clitoris, that's probably why. It's almost as if the feeling is too good for her, so respect her wishes.

Finally, there are points of etiquette for women to remember when receiving cunnilingus:

- Give your partner a chance to breathe! Keep your thighs wide enough apart for him to get some air.
- Cunnilingus is often very exhausting for the tongue muscles after several minutes intense stimulation — so don't be offended if he breaks off for a rest.

fellatio

Fellatio is oral sex performed by a woman on a man or a man on a man. Most men love it — but a few dislike it, or find it brings them to orgasm too quickly.

Ask him first if you wish, but — as with cunnilingus — it might be simpler to go ahead and do it.

What is acceptable fellatio? Well, almost anything really — from kissing and tongue-stroking to actual sucking (with the penis in your mouth). But here are a few hints:

- Do not blow. Despite the common expression 'blow job' (meaning fellatio), it is actually very dangerous to blow down a man's penis, since it can cause serious infection.
- Do not bite! This could cause a nasty injury.
- Try to keep your teeth from touching him as far as possible — men do, quite naturally, feel rather threatened by teeth in this area.

A man will probably try to persuade you to let him climax in your mouth – whether you do is a question of personal preference. Many women simply hate the thought of this. If this applies to you, don't be pressurized: tell him that

Fellatio is very exciting – but it's important to get questions of etiquette sorted out first!

you're going to take him out shortly before he comes.

Many women let their partners climax in the mouth, but won't swallow seminal fluid because they find it distasteful. If that's the way you feel, keep some tissues handy, and dispose of the liquid as soon as you decently can.

Points of etiquette for men receiving fellatio:

- Refrain from thrusting too deeply. After all, how would you like having something the length of a banana rammed so far back into your throat that it makes you gag?
- If your lover wants to stop and take a breather, don't be selfish and urge her to go on — she may badly need the break to relax her mouth.
- Don't pressurize her to let you reach orgasm in her mouth if she doesn't want you to.
- If she does let you come in her mouth, don't expect her to swallow it.

Sexual Fantasies

Most men and women have sexual fantasies — erotic dreams that drift into their minds, particularly while they make love or masturbate. Many people fantasize about their partner, rather than a dream lover, or they have fantasies about an ex-lover, which can cause feelings of guilt. It's common for people to dream about making love to someone of their own sex, and then worry about their sexuality unnecessarily.

While there's no harm in indulging

in fantasy — indeed it can improve your sex life — how much you can safely tell your lover is a question of individual judgement.

Although fantasies are intimate, sharing them with your partner is a good way to make sex more exciting. You should take it in turns to describe what you are imagining or to suggest what fantasy you would like to act out. Different love-making positions can help to make the fantasy come to life. For instance, any position where a man is on top of a woman can help her play out a submission fantasy.

Acting out fantasies is fine as long as your partner is keen too. If one of you likes to do something that distresses the other, you should not pursue it. For instance, some people love dressing up to have sex, but many feel utterly ridiculous doing this. It's a question of finding a balance that you're both comfortable with.

Keep fantasies within your relationship. Bringing others into a fantasy can have disastrous results. For example: someone drunkenly suggests that it would be fun to try three in a bed; it rarely seems such a good idea later when they're sober. The 'realisation' of fantasies like this often ends up hurting several people and should be avoided.

Never reveal your lover's fantasies to someone else without permission. To do so would be to betray a trust that would be very difficult to regain. On the other hand, sharing fantasies with your lover is one of the most intimate and trusting things you can do and it will help to keep a long-term relationship exciting.

keeping sex alive

In long-term sexual relationships sex can get very dull.But it is possible to sleep with one person for the rest of your life if you both work hard to keep things as fresh and lively as possible in bed.

Firstly, if sex is something you confine to the bedroom at night, try making love at different times and in different places. This might be in another room, or while you're having a shower. Equally you might find an appropriate place outside — perhaps in the garden or on a secluded beach. But ensure you aren't going to offend others who might be within earshot.

Try out a different position from time to time.

- This is rather like the position on the opposite page, but communication between the lovers is easier! The man starts by lying flat on his back. The woman now squats astride him, lowering herself on to his penis and then gently moves up and down.

On these and the next pages are some that are comfortable, fun and exciting. Why not try them when you're in the mood?

trying something new

Even if this doesn't work wonders, you are more likely to appreciate the positions you usually adopt when you go back to them.

Some couples find it stimulating to look at themselves in a mirror while they are making love. Another popular way to spice things

• TOP: This comfy position gives good penetration and unusual pressures on the vagina. He lies flat on his back, she kneels astride him facing away, then lowers herself, gently guiding his penis with her hand.

• LEFT: This is good during pregnancy because there is no pressure on the woman's stomach, but it's fun at other times too. She lies on her back with her legs apart and knees drawn up. He enters her from beneath.

up is to watch an erotic video together, or to take sexy photographs of each other.

Treating yourselves to a weekend away can also help, particularly if you have children and you can leave them with someone you trust. Many couples have periods when it's impossible to have good sex because a child

Above: Positions in which the woman sits on the man usually give deep penetration. Here, he sits upright on a bed or floor. She sits on and facing him.

Right: Sometimes called the 'Burgundian', this one demands some athleticism from the woman. It gives deep penetration, but kissing isn't possible.

interrupts the proceedings. It's important to let your partner know if you are finding sex a bit dull or there are aspects of it you're not happy with. Good sex is as much about communication and being on the same emotional wavelength as technique. Bear this in mind when using the techniques given in this book and lasting sexual fulfilment should be achieved.

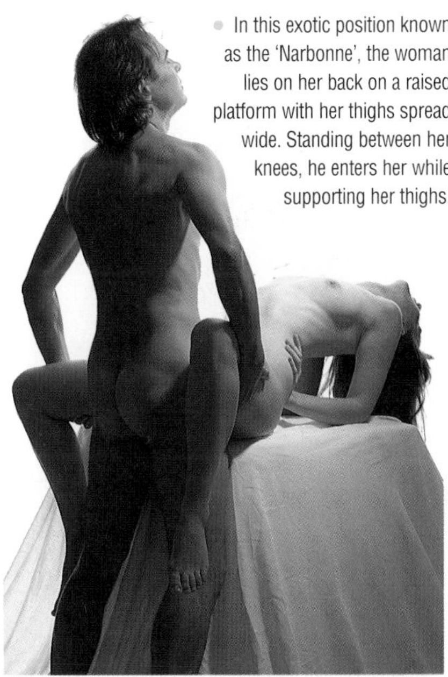

In this exotic position known as the 'Narbonne', the woman lies on her back on a raised platform with her thighs spread wide. Standing between her knees, he enters her while supporting her thighs.

Left: This position gives deep penetration and leaves the hands relatively free to explore each others' bodies. He should sit on a firm surface such as a strong table. She sits on top and facing him, her thighs gripping his.

Various contraception methods

I hope you've enjoyed The Pocket Good Sex Guide! Now, if you're going to put it all into practice, can I urge you to use some sensible method of contraception? Remember that in a marriage or other long-term and loving relationship, a couple should try to decide jointly on what method they're going to use. Various methods are available at present. However, things change rapidly in the field of contraception, and sometimes previously unsuspected side-effects turn up and surprise everybody! So do take a doctor's advice before making up your mind. In Britain, excellent (and free) contraceptive advice is available at Family Planning Clinics, Youth Advisory Clinics and most doctors' surgeries. My thanks to the Family Planning Association for their help with the preparation of this table.

METHOD	HOW IT WORKS	PLUS POINTS	MINUS POINTS
The Condom (male)	Rubber sheath on penis 'catches' sperm.	Easy to buy and use.	Can burst. A few people are allergic to some brands.
Condom (female)	Polyurethane sheath placed in vagina before intercourse.	Like male condom, gives some protection against HIV.	A bit fiddly.Possible for a man to put his penis outside it by mistake.
The Pill	Contains two female hormones which stop the woman ovulating (ie producing eggs).	Helps control heavy/irregular/ painful periods.Reduces chances of some cancers.	Can cause heart attacks or strokes, especially in smokers. May increase risk of some cancers.
The Mini-Pill	Single hormone: thickens womb secretions, making it difficult for sperm to enter womb.	Believed to be safer than the Pill for older women.	Irregular periods common
The Shot	Hormone injection: stops woman ovulating.	One jab gives woman protection for two months (or more).	Periods may become irregular

METHOD	HOW IT WORKS	PLUS POINTS	MINUS POINTS
The vaginal ring	Rubber ring releases hormone into vagina: hormone makes it hard for sperm to enter womb.	Kept in for 3 months; does not interrupt love-making.	Sometimes causes period problems. Long-term effects uncertain.
The implant ('the capsule')	Six tiny rubber capsules put under the skin of woman's arm: they release hormone which stops ovulation.	Protection for five years.	Not easy to remove if you don't like it. Irregular periods common. Long-term effects uncertain.
The IUD (intra-uterine device)	Small plastic and copper object placed in womb; changes womb lining so egg cannot implant itself.	Usually good for long-term protection.	Heavy and sometimes painful periods. Not ideal if you've never had a baby.
The diaphragm	Rubber disc, put into vagina before sex to block sperm. Must have spermicide on it.	May help protect against cancer of the cervix.	Very few. Possibly occasional cases of cystitis.
The sponge	Polyurethane sponge, popped into vagina pre-sex as a barrier. Contains spermicide.	Available from any chemist without prescription.	High pregnancy rate.
Vasectomy	Surgeon cuts through tubes which carry sperm from testicles to penis.	Good permanent method (reversal difficult).	Occasional failures. Some worries about long-term cancer risk.
Female sterilization	Surgeon cuts/blocks tubes which carry eggs to womb.	Another good permanent method. Hard to reverse.	Occasional failures occur.
Natural family planning	You confine sex to woman's 'safe period' — judged by temperature charts and changes in her vaginal mucus.	Acceptable to Catholic church.	Only effective in well-motivated, carefully taught couples.

Index

All page numbers in *italics* are references to illustrations.